INDOOR GARDENING FOR BROWN THUMBS

HANGING PLANTS

by Gary M. Spahl

Illustrated by
Kathleen Estes

BRISTOL PUBLISHING ENTERPRISES
San Leandro, California

Printed in Singapore.

ISBN 1-55867-180-3

CONTENTS

Look for other books
in this series.

Indoor Gardening For Brown Thumbs

HANGING PLANTS
TOUGHEST HOUSEPLANTS
FLOWERING HOUSEPLANTS
HERBS
LARGE FLOOR PLANTS
PLANTS FOR DARK CORNERS

for a free catalog, call or write

Bristol Publishing Enterprises
800 346-4889
in California
510 895-4461
P.O. Box 1737
San Leandro, CA 94577

YOU CAN GROW HANGING PLANTS!

You're surrounded by friends with green thumbs. They're the kind who make everything grow just by looking at it. They bring lush green plants to the office that mock you as they grow vigorously on the corner of the desk. At home, they have lovely feathery greenery hanging in pots in the kitchen window. Trailing vines festoon their bookshelves. Poor you — it seems to be your miserable luck to kill every plant you buy.

No more! This book will help you to grow hanging and trailing plants indoors. You have only to follow the simple directions on the following pages and you will soon develop your own green thumb. In addition to learning the easy steps to keep the plant healthy, you'll find advice on how to hang a plant or make it climb (see **Hanging Out or Training Up**, page 77).

Hanging plants are impressive. The spreading branches covered with leaves are beautiful to look at. The graceful lines lend a sense of calm to our hurried, technologically enhanced lifestyles. And they're versatile. You can train a plant to grow on a trellis or let it all hang out from a pot.

The Age of Aquarius?

Now hanging plants may give you visions of hippies and macramé and herbal tea. Living in California, that stuff doesn't faze me anymore. But trailing tendrils are for *today*. A traditional English Ivy will fit perfectly in a formal dining room. A Wandering Jew can add color to a modern kitchen. Put an Arrowhead Vine in the kids' room for that touch of jungle.

Besides looking good, hanging plants offer the benefits that all houseplants give. All those little leaves act like tiny vacuum cleaners, sucking pollution out of the air. And if you remember grade school science class, plants give off clean, fresh oxygen! Studies have even shown that caring for houseplants can boost your spirits. When your grandmother said she needed to get her hands in the dirt, she knew what she was talking about.

So hanging plants can contribute to keeping you happy and healthy, and this book shows you how to do the same for them. Believe it or not, it doesn't take much effort at all! The eight *Handsome Hanging Plants* described in this book each have different needs, but it only takes a few minutes a week to keep them looking good. Just follow the tips on watering and light, feeding and trimming — and you and your plants will be saying goodbye to that brown thumb!

I know there is a hanging plant, probably more than one, that will be right for you. It will bring natural beauty and warmth into your home. And come to think of it, you might enjoy sipping some herbal tea as you admire that Asparagus Fern.

HANDSOME HANGING PLANTS

In this chapter, find the perfect plant for your personality and the growing conditions in your home, and follow the simple directions to keep it looking good.

This gang of eight* handsome hangers includes a variety of plant styles and growing conditions. There are big, billowy plants and delicate trailing vines. Plants with solid green leaves and others with unique coloring. Some with simple leaves and some with more intricately shaped leaves. Some plants are thirsty and some like things a bit drier. No matter what your decorating needs or how much care you can provide, you'll find a few that will fit your situation.

The illustrations and descriptions in this chapter can help you to recognize a plant and decide if it's for you. Charts with symbols provide quick summaries. The basic care symbols show how much attention a plant requires. Other symbols describe the plant's water and light needs.

*Also, see Pothos in *The Toughest Houseplants, Indoor Gardening for Brown Thumbs*.

BASIC CARE SYMBOLS

 <u>Very Easy Care</u>. If you want a plant that you can almost forget about, look for this symbol.

 <u>Easy Care</u>. If you're willing to give a plant a small amount of care, but still don't want to get too involved, try one marked with this symbol.

 <u>Light Active Care</u>. Plants needing just a little more attention have this symbol.

 <u>Active Care</u>. This plant needs lots of attention.

WATER SYMBOLS

 <u>Dry</u>. These plants like their soil to be fairly dry most of the time. Water every ten days or so, and immediately pour off any water that drains from the bottom.

 <u>Moderate</u>. Most plants fall into this category. The top inch of soil will dry out for a day or two. Once-a-week watering should be fine.

 <u>Wet</u>. Some plants like their soil to be consistently moist. Water weekly and check every few days. Give a light watering if the soil surface feels dry.

LIGHT SYMBOLS

 <u>Low Light</u>. This doesn't mean dark; no plant can live in a closet. You couldn't cast a shadow in low light, but could still read comfortably. This would be fairly close to a north window, or a good distance away from brighter windows.

 <u>Moderate Light</u>. Your best bet for most plants — some distance away from east, west or south windows, or closer if curtains filter the light. You could cast a dim shadow on plants in moderate light.

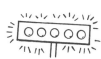 <u>Bright Light</u>. This doesn't necessarily mean full sun. These conditions are found close to east, west and south windows, and there may be times when the area gets direct sunlight. Take care with plants that don't like full sun. Put up a filtering shade, or move the plant out of the sun's path.

Use the charts to help you decide which plants to buy. If you live in a solarium, buy plants that like bright light. If your stack of unread magazines includes articles on whether humans will reach the moon, avoid plants that want some attention.

Each plant also has notes on feeding, trimming, cleaning and pruning. Turn to **More About Plant Care** on page 47 for more information on these topics as well as tips on repotting, propagating and pest control. To learn about how to hang your plant or train it to climb a support, check out **Hanging Out or Training Up** on page 77. But now, go to the next page and read about eight Handsome Hanging Plants.

HEARTLEAF PHILODENDRON

 Very Easy Care

 Moderate

 All Light Conditions

The Heartleaf Philodendron is a graceful, traditional plant that's good for all light conditions. Very easy to grow and propagate. Can trail naturally or be trained to climb an upright form.

Heartleaf Philodendrons first became popular during the Depression, because they were very hardy, propagated quickly and were inexpensive. They really took off in the '50s and '60s. Watch almost any old sitcom or Perry Mason rerun and you'll see one on the set. Of course, these are fake props, but you know something has reached full acceptance in America once it's immortalized in plastic.

Heartleafs are just one of many varieties of Philodendrons, but are the most common because they look so good and are so easy to grow. The two- to four-inch, heart-shaped leaves are smooth, with a cool, dark green color. They grow thickly on long green vines; Heartleaf Philodendrons tend to be quite full.

These plants aren't bold and dramatic. Heartleafs fill their spaces quietly and provide a subtle feeling of calm and order. Still, they're no shrinking violet. They tolerate most light conditions and bad air quality, and grow well with little care. Without pinching or pruning, the vines can get several feet long, although the plant is not a very fast grower.

You can let Heartleafs trail naturally, or wind them loosely around the bottom of your pot or train them to climb. Plant several Heartleafs in the same pot for a better hanging display. Turn to page 77 for tips on training plants. Repot every year or two, when plants are crowded. Repotting information starts on page 63.

Light Requirements for
the Heartleaf Philodendron

You can put this plant anywhere but a sunny window. It likes moderate to bright light, but will also live in low light.

Watering the Heartleaf Philodendron

Water once a week, and let the soil dry a bit between waterings. Be sure to water it thoroughly, and pour off any water left in the drainage saucer after 20 minutes.

Feeding the Heartleaf Philodendron

Feed every three to four months during spring, summer and fall. See page 53 for information about the kinds of fertilizer available. Never exceed the recommendations of the fertilizer manufacturer.

Trimming and Cleaning
the Heartleaf Philodendron

Leaves don't often brown, but can yellow or whither. Remove these weak leaves completely with scissors. Long, lukewarm showers will keep the leaves shiny, and can be considered a thorough watering.

Pinching and Pruning
the Heartleaf Philodendron

Regular pinching and pruning encourages fuller growth. Pinch out new young shoots as they appear. Use sharp scissors to prune long or lanky branches cleanly, leaving a leaf at the end. Turn to page 59 for more on this topic.

Pests and the Heartleaf Philodendron

This plant is resistant to most pests.

For more information about these topics, go to page 47, **More About Plant Care.**

GRAPE IVY

 Easy Care

 Moderate

 Low to Moderate

Grape Ivy is a simple and beautiful choice for low-light situations. Seasonal pruning can keep it from getting straggly. Watch for spider mites and mealy bugs.

A mature Grape Ivy is a thing to behold. The woody stems covered in deep green leaves are reminiscent of a grape arbor. They make me want to mix some lemonade and imagine crickets on a summer night. This is one of the most attractive and easiest hanging plants to grow. Mine has been billowing over a stereo speaker for seven years, flourishing in spite of low light, passive neglect and vibration from my eclectic musical tastes.

Grape Ivy has dark green leaves. Younger leaves have a slightly metallic sheen that makes them look fresh and vibrant; older leaves develop a light fuzz on the underside. It seems we're not the only ones who grow hair in weird places as we age. A close relative, known as a *Kangaroo Vine*, grows under similar conditions and care, but has lighter, more oval leaves with more intricately scalloped edges.

The branches of this plant can get as long as six feet. Pinching out new growth helps plants stay bushy and compact; with occasional trims they grow fairly long and full. Repot plants about every year or two. See page 63 for more about repotting.

Light Requirements for Grape Ivy
This plant can live in a dim corner or in moderate light.

Watering Grape Ivy

Let soil get slightly dry between waterings. Water every seven to ten days or so, and pour excess drainage water out of the saucer after 20 minutes.

Feeding Grape Ivy

During spring, summer and fall, feed every three to four months. See page 53 for information about the kinds of fertilizer available. Never exceed the recommendations of the fertilizer manufacturer.

Trimming and Cleaning Grape Ivy

Scissors can be used to trim browning edges, following the leaf's natural line. Remove leaves that are difficult to trim naturally. Remove yellow or withered leaves close to the main stem. Occasional showers will keep the plant looking fresh.

Pinching and Pruning Grape Ivy

Regular pinching and pruning encourages fuller growth (see page 59 for more information). Pinch out young branch tips as they appear. Use sharp scissors to prune long or lanky branches cleanly. If the branch is young, prune back to a healthy leaf. Prune weak, woody stalks to the top of the soil or the originating branch.

Pests and Grape Ivy

Grape Ivy is susceptible to spider mites and mealy bugs. Regular misting or spraying with insecticides can control mites, but they are difficult to eliminate. Use insecticide to control mealy bugs. Read more about pests and pest control on page 72.

For more information about all of these subjects, go to page 47, **More About Plant Care**.

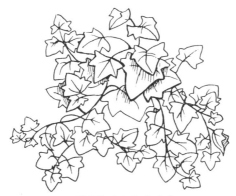

HEDERA IVY

Easy Care

Moderate

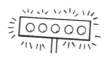

Bright, Some Sun

Hedera Ivy is a classic — elegant and very attractive. Many varieties. Can be trained on forms for lots of decorating options. Fairly easy to grow and propagate, but watch for pests.

Mention the word *ivy* and what do you think of? Probably the Ivy League — old brick buildings filled with books and covered in hundred-year-old vines. Or you might think of British period films with grand costumes and formal teas. Ivy has that dignified feeling. Maybe it's because the leaves are found on many coats-of-arms, or maybe it's just cultural training. If ivy grew on fast food joints instead of pricey colleges, we might have a whole different image of burger palaces.

There are many varieties of Hedera Ivy. The most common is *English Ivy*, which has rich emerald green leaves that are two to four inches long, with three to five lobes. Leaves of other varieties can range from one-half inch to six inches across. The dramatic *Canary Island Ivy*, for example, has large leaves thickly edged with white. Hedera Ivy leaves can be curled or wavy, and can have mottled markings or edging in white, cream, yellow or pink.

Hedera Ivy, unlike most houseplants, is not a tropical plant. It is a strong (indeed, invasive in some situations) grower in the outdoors, but because of its popularity has been developed for indoor conditions by growers. Indoors it is quite hardy, and cuttings can grow for some time in water. It can get straggly, so regular pinching is a good idea. You can also train it to climb (see page 77). These plants like things a bit cramped, so repot only when roots have filled the pot, about every two years. Page 63 provides tips on repotting.

Light Requirements for Hedera Ivy
Set these plants in spaces that get bright light, with several hours of direct sun each day. More light produces better markings.

Watering Hedera Ivy
Keep the soil barely moist. Water thoroughly every week or so, and pour out water from the drainage saucer after 20 minutes.

Feeding Hedera Ivy
During spring, summer and fall, feed every three to four months. See page 53 for information about the kinds of fertilizer available. Never exceed the recommendations of the fertilizer manufacturer.

Trimming and Cleaning Hedera Ivy
Trim browning sections from larger leaves with scissors, following the leaf's natural shape. On plants with smaller leaves, it's easier to just remove those that are browning. Remove any yellow or withered leaves. Lukewarm showers keep the plant clean and healthy, and also serve as a good watering, if the soil is soaked.

Pinching and Pruning Hedera Ivy

Pinching and pruning encourages fuller growth. Pinch out new branch tips periodically, but limit pinching if you want longer vines. Prune back long or lanky branches to a healthy leaf. More information begins on page 59.

Pests and Hedera Ivy

Hedera Ivy is susceptible to pests, especially spider mites, mealy bugs and whiteflies. Regular misting or spraying with insecticides can control mites. Use insecticide to control mealy bugs and whiteflies. Mites and whiteflies are difficult to eliminate. See page 72 for more about pests and pest control.

Go to page 47, **More About Plant Care**, for more information about all of these topics.

ARROWHEAD VINE

Easy Care

Moderate

Bright

The bright, cheery Arrowhead Vine grows quickly with very little care. Regular pinching will create a more compact, shapely plant. Very easy to propagate.

This plant could turn me into a vegetarian. An Arrowhead's leaves are so bright and fresh that every time I see one, I want to make a salad. You'll sometimes find these in malls and lobbies where there is bright light and their fast growth is well-managed. A heavily pruned plant will keep throwing its leaves upright in a broad burst. If left to trail, Arrowhead Vines can grow up to six feet long.

Whether climbing a trellis, pinched back to stay bushy or left to grow long and wild, these are attractive plants. Young leaves are about three inches long and — surprise! — shaped like an arrowhead. The basic variety has dark green leaves with silvery markings on the veins. As the plant matures, the leaves split into multiple leaflets and lose the markings. The leaves of the *Imperial White* variety are a bright blend of green and white, with dark green edges. This plant's leaves keep the arrowhead shape as they mature.

Like their Philodendron cousins, Arrowheads are very easy to grow. The only real attention they need is regular pinching back of vine tips to keep the plant shapely and protect your house from being overtaken. Repot them about every year or two. See page 63 for repotting tips.

Light Requirements for the Arrowhead Vine

Put the Arrowhead Vine in a spot that gets

moderate to bright light, but keep it away from direct sun.

Watering the Arrowhead Vine

This plant likes its soil to be kept barely moist, so water every five to seven days. Pour drainage water out of the saucer after 20 minutes. Avoid letting soil dry completely.

Feeding the Arrowhead Vine

Feed every two to three months during spring, summer and fall. Fertilize less often to control growth. Never exceed the amount of fertilizer recommended by the manufacturer. See page 53 for information about the kinds of fertilizer available.

Trimming and Cleaning the Arrowhead Vine

Trim browning sections with scissors, following the leaf's natural shape. Remove any yellow or withered leaves at the main stem. Lukewarm showers keep the plant clean and, if the soil is soaked, serve as a good watering.

Pinching and Pruning the Arrowhead Vine

Pinch back stem tips to encourage branching and create better leaf markings. Prune straggly or long branches to a healthy leaf or to the plant's base. See page 59 for detailed information on this topic.

Pests and the Arrowhead Vine

Arrowhead Vines are resistant to most pests.

For more information about these subjects, go to page 47, **More About Plant Care.**

CREEPING FIG

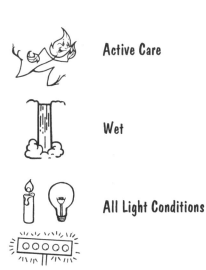

Active Care

Wet

All Light Conditions

The Creeping Fig is handsome and delicate, and needs lots of attention. It's a good choice for people who overwater. Sensitive to drafts and temperature changes. Watch for spider mites.

Don't judge a book by its cover, or a plant by its sweet-sounding name. The Creeping Fig is probably the most demanding of the eight hanging plants. It could benefit from my Polish grandmother, who always filled us kids up with food and dressed us so heavily against the cold we could barely move. If you've got grandmotherly tendencies, then you'll get along fine with this thirsty, sensitive, but very pretty plant.

Compared to other trailing plants, Creeping Figs are rather dainty. The wiry vines only get about two feet long. They are covered with one- to three-inch, slightly heart-shaped leaves that are a shiny Kelly green. *Creeping* is a good word to describe them. While other hanging plants seem to leap out of their pots on long vines that could support Tarzan, this plant spreads steadily across the soil and eventually trickles down the side of its pot. This creeping growth makes it more suitable for lower spaces than for hanging from high perches.

This plant likes moist conditions, with lots of water and humidity. If the soil dries out, the leaves can wilt and they won't revive. Creeping Figs are also sensitive to drafts or sudden temperature changes, which can make the leaves fall off (although they will usually come back). While they do need frequent watering, they prefer to be a bit cramped — you can forget about repotting for three or four years! More about repotting appears on page 63.

Light Requirements for the Creeping Fig

A Creeping Fig can live happily in a spot that gets moderate or fairly bright light. It also tolerates lower light, but leaves will have a darker color.

Watering the Creeping Fig

This plant likes to be kept moist. Water thoroughly every five to seven days and check soil every few days. Plants in brighter light may need more frequent watering. Pour out water left in the drainage saucer after 20 minutes.

Feeding the Creeping Fig

Feed every two to three months during spring, summer and fall. See page 53 for information about the kinds of fertilizer available. Never exceed the recommendations of the fertilizer manufacturer.

Trimming and Cleaning the Creeping Fig

Trim browning sections with scissors, following the leaf's natural shape. Remove yellow or withered leaves at the main stem. A lukewarm shower will keep the leaves shiny and can replace a regular watering.

Pinching and Pruning the Creeping Fig

Regular pinching controls growth and encourages fullness. Pinch out young branch tips as they appear. Prune long or lanky branches back to a healthy leaf. See page 59 for more on this topic.

Pests and the Creeping Fig

The Creeping Fig is susceptible to spider mites. Regular misting or spraying with insecticides can control mites, but they're difficult to eliminate. Turn to page 72 for more about pests and pest control.

For more information about all of these subjects, go to page 47, **More About Plant Care**.

BUTTON FERN

 Light Active Care

 Wet

 Low to Moderate

The Button Fern is a small, pretty plant that needs a little extra care. The leaf pattern gives it a whimsical personality. Good for people who overwater. Can go years without repotting.

One summer I worked in a factory, removing plastic forks and spoons from the poured forms. You just twisted each utensil off the line of plastic — again and again. The Button Fern reminds me of this job, with its round leaves growing on either side of stiff fronds — left, right, left, right. Compared to the free-wheeling spirit of other trailing plants, this plant's growth pattern is very symmetrical, making it perfect for engineers, accountants and others who need order in their lives. For the rest of us, the gracefully trailing fronds provide a natural feel.

Button Ferns are small plants; the fronds get no longer than a foot. (Fern branches are called fronds. I don't know why; they just are.) The young, dark green leaves are about the size and shape of a shirt button. The leaves get more oval or oblong as they mature. Like other trailing plants with stiff branches, the leaves' weight eventually weighs the fronds down, giving them a nice arching appearance.

This dainty-looking plant needs a little extra care. You might think the leathery leaves can handle dry conditions, but this plant likes to be kept moist. Occasional misting will provide extra humidity. The root mass doesn't grow quickly and the Button Fern likes to be a bit cramped, so it only needs repotting every three or four years. Page 63 provides more repotting tips.

Light Requirements for the Button Fern

A Button Fern does well in low to moderate light.

Watering the Button Fern

Keep soil constantly moist during spring, summer and fall. Water every five to seven days and pour off drainage water after 20 minutes. Check soil every few days; the top should always feel moist. Let the soil dry a bit in winter. Weekly waterings should be fine.

Feeding the Button Fern

Feed every six to eight weeks during spring, summer and fall. See page 53 for information about the kinds of fertilizer available. Never exceed the recommendations of the fertilizer manufacturer.

Trimming and Cleaning the Button Fern

The leaves are too small to trim. Remove unattractive or unhealthy leaves at the frond. Give the plant a lukewarm shower to keep it clean.

Pinching and Pruning the Button Fern

A Button Fern frond won't branch or continue growing if pinched. Prune weak or unattractive fronds back to the soil, rather than cutting only partially, to avoid short, awkward-looking fronds.

Pests and the Button Fern

Button Ferns are susceptible to mealy bugs. Use insecticides to control them. Turn to page 72 for more about pests and pest control.

For more information about all of these subjects, go to page 47, **More About Plant Care**.

ASPARAGUS FERN

Active Care

Moderate

Moderate to Bright

The Asparagus Fern is one of the most dramatic hanging plants. Tolerates sunny locations. Fast-growing roots need special attention. Watch for aphids and spider mites.

It's not asparagus, and it's not really a fern, either. Ferns have fronds; this plant has branches. But it's a very impressive plant. As the branches of this plant grow, they produce an abundance of tiny green leaves that give the plant a light, feathery appearance.

There are several varieties of the Asparagus Fern. One has somewhat upright branches that grown to reach 18 to 24 inches, eventually cascading over from their own weight. Another has branches that grow over the side of the pot and hang, becoming as long as four to five feet. In some varieties, at each junction where a secondary branch grows from the main branch, the Asparagus Fern produces a tiny, very sharp thorn. Color ranges from lemony green to emerald green, depending on the variety. Big and billowing, Asparagus Ferns have the airy quality of a cloud, just not one you'd want to rest your head on.

Occasionally the Asparagus Fern produces round berries, which are toxic.

You'll know this plant is not happy by showers of falling yellow leaves. The truth is, it is a bit messy even when it is happy, but it's worth it. It's important to watch the fast-growing, fleshy roots. They can fill a pot within months and make watering difficult. Repot plants before they get to this state. Always plant the Asparagus Fern two inches below the container's rim to allow the roots room to push up the soil. You can also trim the roots with a sharp knife to keep a plant in the same pot. See page 63 for more information about repotting.

Light Requirements for the Asparagus Fern

The Asparagus Fern will do best in moderate to bright light. It can tolerate some direct sun.

Watering the Asparagus Fern

Weekly waterings should be fine. Pour water out of the drainage saucer after 20 minutes. Keep the soil barely moist and avoid letting it dry out completely.

Feeding the Asparagus Fern

Fertilize from spring through fall, using a time-release fertilizer or fertilizer diluted in the weekly watering. Never exceed the recommendations of the fertilizer manufacturer. See page 53 for detailed information about fertilizer. Limit feeding to limit growth.

Trimming and Cleaning the Asparagus Fern

Carefully give the branches a little shake to remove yellow leaves (be ready with the vacuum cleaner). Trim yellowing branches back to the remaining healthy portion, or back to the soil. Handle the branches with care to avoid being pierced with the sharp thorns. Occasional showers will keep the plant looking fresh.

Pinching and Pruning the Asparagus Fern

Branches are tough and most varieties are prickly. Using scissors and gloves, cut stem ends or prune long branches to encourage bushy growth. Prune unhealthy branches back to the soil.

Pests and the Asparagus Fern

The Asparagus Fern is susceptible to spider mites. Regular misting or spraying with insecticides can control mites, but they are difficult to eliminate. Read more about pests and pest control on page 72.

For more information about all of these subjects, go to page 47, **More About Plant Care.**

WANDERING JEW

Easy Care

Moderate

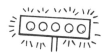

Bright, Some Sun

The Wandering Jew is a fast-growing, colorful plant with long trailing branches. Easy to propagate. Needs bright light for best color.

These are the beauty queens of the eight hanging plants. Wandering Jews are popular because they grow and propagate easily, and offer a variety of choices. Some plants are mostly green with thin white stripes. Another variety has black-purple leaves with light purple stripes. Some have green leaves with silver markings and purple undersides. Other colors include purplish-red and bronze.

These plants are subtle; they wear their colors well. They're not flashy and over-dressed. Wandering Jews need lots of light to develop good color. They'll tolerate lower light, but the leaves will turn a solid green. Also known as *Inch Plants*, they have one- to three-inch, pointed oval leaves growing on fleshy stems that can reach several feet in length. The leaves are very soft — they can rot with overwatering and burn in too much sun. Watch the leaves closely until you get a sense of what works for the plant.

Wandering Jews grow quickly, but they can get straggly and don't age well. Frequent pinching keeps a plant full. After a few years, propagate new plants from cuttings (see page 67) and put the old plant on the compost heap. Repot when the roots get crowded, about every year or so. See page 63 for information about repotting plants.

Light Requirements for the Wandering Jew

Put this plant in a spot that gets bright light, even a few hours of direct sun. Brighter light will produce more vibrant leaf colors.

Watering the Wandering Jew

Let the soil dry out a bit between waterings. Water once a week, and pour excess water out of the drainage saucer after 20 minutes.

Feeding the Wandering Jew

Feed every two to three months from spring to fall. See page 53 for information about fertilizer. To control growth, fertilize every four to six months. Never exceed the recommendations of the fertilizer manufacturer.

Trimming and Cleaning the Wandering Jew

This plant's leaves are so small they're not worth trimming; remove leaves that look yellow or unattractive. Occasional showers will keep the plant clean and, if the soil is soaked, serve as a good watering.

Pinching and Pruning the Wandering Jew

Use fingernails to pinch off stem tips just above a healthy leaf. This will encourage fuller growth. Prune long or straggly branches back to a healthy leaf, or to the soil. For more information about pinching and pruning, see page 59.

Pests and the Wandering Jew
This plant is resistant to most pests.

Additional information about all of these subjects is provided in **More About Plant Care**, beginning on page 47.

HOW TO CHOOSE
A HANGING PLANT

Searching for a Soulmate

You and your plants need to get along. They should please you and you should keep them alive. Ideally, you'll have your plants for a long time, so look at buying them the way you look at a relationship.

You know what happens when dating starts to get serious. You look across the table and ask yourself: Do I like this person? How much? Does my busy workload mesh with his part-time job passing out mini-franks at the Superette? How will he look snoring on my sofa every Sunday? The answers to these questions (honest answers) help you decide if the two of you should forge ahead.

Because you'll have the most success with a plant that matches your schedule, lifestyle and home environment, ask the same kinds of questions. When you're gazing across the greenhouse aisle into that Button Fern's eyes, ask yourself: Where would I put this? Is there enough space? Enough light? Does it match my decor? Would I remember to water it? Do I have time to care for a needy plant?

Does This Thing Come With Instructions?

Take a copy of this book along. Or hunt for care tags attached to plants; they can really help. If the tag says a plant needs sun, don't buy it if you don't have windows. If a plant needs water every few days, pass it by if you can't remember to bring in your mail. There's no need to set yourself up for failure by choosing something that won't fit into your life.

In the end, if all of the answers seem right, and you like the plant, buy it. Follow the incredibly easy instructions in this book and you won't go wrong.

I know a lady who brings home any plant that appeals to her, and tries it out. She operates on the assumption that either it gets along with her system or it gets tossed. She waters once a week, adding fertilizer to the water.

Occasionally she showers and trims the plants. She figures that she has a better than 50% success rate.

Now that seems to me the expensive way, not to mention frustrating. Better to have your ducks in a row before you start.

YOUR HANDY PLANT SHOPPING GUIDE
Good Choice

- Even growth, good shape
- Dense foliage

- Loose, moist soil
- Crisp, green leaves

Poor Choice

- Lanky and straggly
- Yellow, wilted or torn leaves
- Sparse, uneven foliage

- Dry, hard or mildewy soil
- Evidence of pests
- Thick, visible roots

Buyer Beware

What do you do when you pick up a peach in the store and it's bruised, brown and mushy? You say "Yuk!" and put it back. It's the same with houseplants. You want one that's healthy and attractive. You're not getting a plant to give it a facelift or nurse it to health.

Much of this is common sense. Choose a plant that looks good and avoid those that

seem like they've just sur-
vived the Hong Kong flu.
Make sure the soil is moist
and loose in the pot, and
that no roots are visible at
the top or through the
drainage holes. Check for
signs of pests and disease
such as white spots,
brown spots, tiny webs or
bugs. If the plants in a store

> **fungus/leaf mold:** fungus diseases can result from too much water on leaves, creating brown or black spots, or a gray, fluffy mold on leaves and stems.

don't seem healthy or well cared for, look
someplace else.

Go for the Effect; Then Look at Price

With the exception of exotic varieties,
houseplants are quite affordable. Most starter
plants are sold in four- to six-inch pots and
usually cost under $6.00. You may, however,
want a hanging plant that is a bit larger. You
can get a Wandering Jew in a four-inch pot, but
it will take awhile to fill the bay window. It may
cost a little more, but a big part of a hanging
plant's appeal is the full, trailing effect. It's
worth the few extra dollars to buy a plant that
will look good right away. Why buy a hanging
plant that won't hang for a year?

Hanging plants in eight- or ten-inch pots
can range from $6.00 to $15.00. The difference is where the plant is purchased. A discount store may have an Asparagus Fern for

$6.99. It may cost $9.99 at a greenhouse, and $12.99 at a florist. Look for the best quality at the lowest price. Don't worry about status; no one's going to ask where you bought the plant.

It's Hard To Be the New Kid on the Block

Always keep a new plant away from other plants for a few weeks. Even if you've checked for pests and disease, you may have missed

IT ONLY TAKES A FEW MINUTES

The trip from the greenhouse to your house can set the stage for a plant's untimely demise. Almost all houseplants are tropical plants. A minute or two of exposure to winter air can shock a plant — and it may never recover. If you're buying a plant during cold weather, make sure it's wrapped or bagged for the trip to and from the car. Summer heat can also damage plants. Never leave a plant in a hot car. You could come back to find it wilted — permanently.

something. If a new Creeping Fig with spider mites sits next to a healthy Grape Ivy, you can bet those mites will get a quick taste for grape juice. If a new plant seems healthy after a few weeks, you can place it near the other plants and let them bond.

MORE ABOUT PLANT CARE

Water

Water Is Life — Period!

We need eight glasses of water a day to keep our bodies healthy. Plants need water too! It's like a plant's blood, carrying nutrients to all its body parts. It's a mystery that we don't usually drink enough water, but we want our plants to drink too much! We're more likely to overwater a plant than underwater it.

How to Water

Plants don't drink every day, so water them thoroughly. The roots need to take up enough water to support the whole plant. Don't just dribble a few spoonfuls from your watering can while you go from plant to plant whistling a tune. You might as well play a funeral dirge.

Pour water over the surface of the soil until it comes out of the pot's drainage holes. Make sure there's something underneath to catch the drainage. It may be a good idea to take hanging plants down when you water them. Those lush vines can make your den look like the rain forest, but you can do without the rain on your carpet.

After 20 minutes, the soil and roots have

absorbed as much as they can. Dump out any water left in the drainage pan because it can cause the roots to rot.

Nothin' Wrong with Plain Old H₂O

Tap water is fine for most plants. It should feel pleasantly warm, like a summer rain. Cold water can shock plants. If you know you have chlorine in your water, set some in an open

IT'S NOT THE HEAT, IT'S THE HUMIDITY

Some plants, including the Creeping Fig and Button Fern, like extra moisture in the air. Misting plants with water will increase humidity, but do it early in the day. Water left on leaves during cool evenings can cause disease. Grouping plants together allows them to share moisture; each plant takes in water that evaporates from the others. You can also set plants on shallow trays filled with pebbles and water, which will evaporate and increase humidity. Or put plants in the kitchen or bathroom, the most humid rooms in the house.

container overnight to let the chlorine evaporate. Water softeners use chemicals that can damage plants, so if you have one, use cheap bottled water from a gallon jug instead.

Zen and the Art of Watering Houseplants?

A friend of mine has a unique theory about watering plants: when they're lying down and gasping, it's time to water. Needless to say, he doesn't have many healthy plants. You can't meditate and hope for intuition, either. Water a plant when it needs water.

Learn what your plant likes. Use weekly watering as a baseline, and increase or decrease the frequency based on the plant's needs. Depending on room temperature, light and other considerations, the soil will stay moist for some time and the plant will take a sip when it's thirsty.

To check a plant to see if it needs water, stick your finger into the soil about an inch. If it feels fairly moist, it's probably okay. If it's dry, it's time to water. Or pick up the plant and "weigh" it in your hand. If it feels heavy, the soil probably has enough moisture. If it feels light, time to water. If the leaves look droopy or feel limp, *and* the soil feels dry, it's probably thirsty. But don't use my friend's method, because that's living too much on the edge.

CRIES FOR HELP

- Growth slows
- Leaves wilt or become limp
- Lower leaves curl, yellow or fall off
- Leaf edges turn brown and dry

- Leaves get soft, rotten patches
- Leaves curl, yellow and tips turn brown
- Young and old leaves fall off
- Leaf growth is poor

Thirsty plants and waterlogged plants have some similar symptoms. Put your finger into the soil to be sure about the condition causing the symptoms.

The Goldilocks Approach

Just like the porridge at the Three Bears' house, water your plants not too little, not too much, but just right. Use moderation. And if you're not sure if it's time to water, wait another day or so. It's always better to underwater than overwater.

Light

No Light, No Action

I'm not going to get into a long scientific discussion about chlorophyll and photosynthesis, but I will say that plants do something pretty amazing with light. They turn it into

---

SHUT THE DOOR!
WERE YOU BORN IN A BARN?

Did you ever get so cold you couldn't warm up? Or so hot you felt dizzy? Plants are sensitive to temperature changes, and less likely to recover. Keep plants away from doors and drafty windows. A cold wind from someone walking in the door might chill you, but it can send a plant into shock.

Another tip: Be careful with plants near heating elements. You may buy a plant in the summer, set it near a heating register or vent and it will look beautiful, until those cold, autumn nights when you've cranked up the heat. You might find your soft, supple plant has become crispy.

CRIES FOR HELP

IT'S TOO DARK IN HERE!

- New leaves small, pale
- Stems elongated between leaves
- Less vibrant colors
- Dropping leaves

HOW ABOUT A LITTLE SHADE?

- Mature leaves pale, washed out
- Stems and leaves droop
- Burned patches on leaves
- Dropping leaves

food! Don't ask me how, just trust me. Or ask any sixth grader.

Since light is a food source, plants need the right amount. Too much can turn leaves pale or even burn them. Not enough can make a plant small and spindly. The poor thing will stretch for whatever weak light it can find, not unlike the way a desperate dieter stretches for that package of Oreos hidden behind the rice cakes.

Location, Location, Location

Some plants can live in low light; others need full sun. The light you can provide depends on how much comes in through the windows. And once light enters a room, it can be magnified or swallowed up. A light-colored room will be brighter because it reflects the light; a room with dark colors will absorb light and be darker. You thought this was just your imagination.

So it's important to find the right spot for your plant, from a lighting perspective. That Asparagus Fern might brighten up the dark corner in the family room, but without more light you'll soon be looking at an empty dark corner again.

Some houseplants are natives of the jungle, where they grow in the shade of taller trees. So bright light isn't right for every plant. Of the eight Handsome Hanging Plants, only the Creeping Fig and the Asparagus Fern like constant bright light. Just like watering, you can give a plant too much of a good thing.

One Good Turn Deserves Another

Because plants need light, they grow toward it. Maybe this is why people at parties congregate in the kitchen — they need food! To help plants grow evenly, give them an occasional turn — a quarter- or half-turn every few days or once a week is enough. It depends on how quickly the plant grows. You'll know to give the old ivy a whirl when it's leaning perilously to one side.

Fertilizer

Strap on the Feedbag!

Living in California, where everyone is beautiful, the lifestyle police check to make sure you're eating a healthy diet. Still, I'm a big fan of vitamins, and I notice the difference when I don't take them. While plants get food from light and soil, fertilizer acts like vitamins by providing additional nutrients. We can live without taking vitamins, and plants will survive without fertilizer. But without those extra nutrients, we both might be a bit less healthy.

The best fertilizer for foliage (non-flowering) plants has a balanced blend of minerals, which is listed on the package by three iden-

---

WELCOME HOME TO A DIET

Plants you buy have been eating like Olympic athletes. They're fed lots of fertilizer so they'll grow quickly and get to market faster. Because houseplants are raised under ideal conditions, they can handle the extra food. But unless you live in a greenhouse, home conditions can't support the extra nutrients. Flush fertilizer out of new plants by running water through the soil in the sink. If a pot holds one quart of water, flush it with two quarts. Don't feed a new plant for at least four months. Given the shock of moving, it won't be hungry for awhile.

---

tical numbers such as 20-20-20. This means there are equal amounts of nitrogen (for active growth), phosphate (for strong roots) and potassium (for healthy leaves).

Lots of Flavors to Choose From

Houseplant food comes in liquids, powders, pellets and time-release sticks. Liquid and powdered fertilizer are mixed with water. Time-release sticks and pellets are put into or on top of the soil and release a little food with each watering. Fish emulsion liquid is a good natural fertilizer that doesn't include chemicals (but it's a bit odorous). Fertilizer is available at plant, discount and hardware stores. Read the package instructions and choose the type that best fits your level of effort. As for me, I pop in some time-release sticks once a year and the kitchen's closed.

There's Nothing Like Moderation

You can give a plant too much light — too much water — and too much fertilizer. There are good reasons to limit fertilizing. First, feeding a plant steadily will make it grow. It can get too big for its location. You'll have to prune them. It will need regular repotting. Less food, less growth, less effort — a simple equation. Limiting fertilizer isn't just a matter of controlling growth; you can literally overfeed plants.

> ## AVOID WINTER WEIGHT SYNDROME
> When I lived in New England, we'd all eat heavily in the winter, and then rush to diet in the warmer months so we'd look good in bathing suits. With plants it's just the opposite. You should cut their diet in the fall and winter, when they're in a low-growth or dormant period. Avoid fertilizing plants from October to March. Let up on the water, too. In spring and summer, when plants are actively growing, they can return to eating and drinking with controlled abandon.

When fertilizer minerals dissolve in water, they can burn a plant.

Consider mixing fertilizer solutions at one-half or even one-quarter of the recommended strength. Put in less than what's recommended for time-release fertilizer, too. Always check a plant's individual needs. Slow growing plants need less food than active ones. Plants in low light also need less food. Remember, with fertilizer, less is more.

Trimming and Cleaning

A Little Spring (or Any Season) Cleaning

When I owned a car, I used to spend one spring and fall afternoon getting the thing in shape. I didn't open the hood; that's what mechanics are for. But I'd clean out all the bits of trash, wash the windows inside and out, polish the seats and dashboard. For a month or so it felt like a new car, at least on the inside.

It's important to do the same for plants. Even if you take perfect care of them, they can benefit from a little sprucing up every now and then. It's amazing how much better a plant looks after you trim withered, yellow and browning leaves and wash away the dust. Plus it keeps them healthy and more resistant to pests and disease.

Trimming

It's pretty easy to trim the Handsome Hanging Plants. Since most of them have small leaves, just remove unattractive ones. Withered and yellowing leaves should definitely be removed since they are weak and drain the plant's energy. Cut leaves back to the branch or the soil with scissors.

If there are browning patches on small leaves, such as on a Wandering Jew, just take the leaves off. They're too small to trim. But for the larger leaves of an Arrowhead Vine, for example, use scissors to trim away any brown areas. Follow the leaf's natural line. For a Heartleaf Philodendron's pointed oval shape, trim from the center of the leaf up toward the tip, maintaining the oval curve. You'll probably need to cut away some healthy sections to keep the leaf even. Done properly, a trimmed leaf should look like a smaller version of the original.

Cleaning

A houseplant is a living thing. It not only eats and drinks, it also breathes! You can get away without cleaning the dust off your coffee table and it will just look a little grayer. But if you don't remove dust and grime from your plants, you could slowly suffocate them. A plant with dusty leaves is like a person with a stuffed-up nose.

THEN THERE'S REALLY PERSONAL CARE

Some people think playing soft music helps plants grow, and that loud music hurts them. My plants live through everything from Mozart to Motown to angst-driven, Euro-synth pop. I say play what you like; plants will adapt. I'm not playing Gregorian chants to keep my Ivy happy — it would stress me out. Then there's the theory that talking to or naming your plants is a good idea. It certainly can't hurt them, and it probably provides calming benefits for you. If the plants start talking back, get some help.

The easiest way to clean hanging plants is with a light shower. Did you catch the emphasis on the word *light*? Most houseplants are natives of the tropics, but they don't fare too well in hurricanes and monsoons. Create a soft jungle rain. You can do this with the kitchen sink sprayer, or put the plant in the shower. If you have a massage setting on your shower head, don't even think about it!

Think of the Goldilocks approach for water temperature: not too hot, not too cold, but just right. Be sure to clean both sides of the leaves; it's like scrubbing behind your ears. Just turn the branches under the stream and let the water wash all the plant's troubles away.

Pinching and Pruning

You've Got to be Cruel to be Kind

You know the old wives' tale that if you shave your hair it will grow back faster and thicker. This isn't true for people, but the theory does work for plants. You've probably seen arborists hanging in a big old tree and pruning off branches. When they're done, the tree often looks shockingly bare, and you wonder why they did such a hack job. Weeks later you'll look up and notice that a lot of growth has come back, and that the tree looks fuller and healthier!

This is part of nature's wonder: plants are

compelled to grow. Trees can be stripped bare in a hurricane, fields can be left barren after a wildfire. But within a few weeks the rejuvenation process begins, and new growth appears. Most pinching and pruning isn't this drastic. But if you cut branches of an Asparagus Fern back to the soil, new shoots will sprout up and you'll soon have a vigorous new plant.

Pinching

Left on their own, trailing vines and branches just keep growing longer. Pinching out branch tips will create a more attractive plant with many branches and denser growth. With your fingernails, just remove young growing tips, right down to where a leaf begins. Some plants will send out two new shoots where the tip was removed, so the one branch will continue as two. Other plants may sprout new growth where older leaves join the branch.

How much pinching you do depends on how bushy you want the plant, how long you want the vines and how quickly it grows. Frequent pinching creates a very full but short plant. Occasional pinching provides less dense growth, but lets the branches grow longer. It's always best to pinch while plants are actively growing, so they can put energy into new growth. Pinching works well for the Heartleaf Philodendron, Grape Ivy, Hedera Ivy, Arrowhead Vine and Wandering Jew.

Pruning

Every spring I wade into my Grape Ivy with a pair of scissors. I prune the tips and cut away straggly branches. When the job is finished, I have to admit the plant looks a bit airy. But after a few weeks — while I've been paying attention to things like taxes and pruning my own winter weight — I notice that new, robust shoots are sprouting. My trusty Grape will soon be the lush green specimen I know and love.

Think of pruning as an advanced version of pinching; you're just removing more of the plant. You might prune a plant to cut away older or bare branches. Or to help it fit into a certain space. Or to remove a branch that's growing in a weird direction.

Go for the Natural Look

Before you prune, get a sense of the plant's overall shape and growth pattern. Professional tree trimmers don't hack branches off willy-nilly. Remember, you're removing parts of the plant to get it to grow. If you prune away all the branches on one side, the plant is going to grow lopsided. Prune a plant to keep it looking natural. And give up any notion of shaping it into a farm animal; you're not doing topiary.

Pruning often involves cutting into older growth, and it's pretty traumatic to have a limb cut in half or removed. Use sharp scissors or pruning shears to make clean cuts and avoid bruising the plant. Remove sections that look weak or old. These branches won't regain their youthful vigor, and the plant wastes energy trying to keep older growth going. Cut back to the closest area of healthy growth, just at the point where a leaf or other branch is attached. Or cut back to the soil. Once the old growth is gone, prune other branches to give the plant a nice, even shape.

It's better to prune while a plant is actively growing or just before it wakes from its winter snooze. Don't be afraid to be brutal; new growth will appear. If you feel guilty, save some of the healthier prunings to propagate into new plants. (See page 67 for information about propagating.)

Repotting

Getting New Digs

You know what it's like to move. It's a hassle, it's messy — but when everything's put away and you've settled in, it's worth it. Repotting means moving a plant into another, usually larger, pot. This provides nutrients from fresh soil, and gives the roots room to grow. It can be a messy process for people, and just as traumatic for a plant. But once the plant has adjusted to its new pot, it will be much happier.

You can tell a plant needs repotting if the soil dries out more quickly than usual between waterings. If roots are coming out of the pot's drainage holes, or you can see roots the size of carrots through the holes, the plant's pot-bound. This is not a good thing. Go to a shoe store, try on shoes that are one size too small, and you'll get an idea of what being pot-bound feels like. A pot-bound plant will have lackluster growth, and eventually die from lack of nutrients and oxygen to the roots.

It's best to repot in the early spring. The plant will use the nutrients and room to start a season of healthy growth. General guidance says to repot every year or so. I keep my plants in their pots a bit longer and they do okay. Part of this is laziness, I must admit. But another reason is space management. Keeping plants

in smaller pots can control growth. If you buy an English Ivy because it looks good in that small alcove, you'd better have a new neighborhood in mind if you keep repotting it. Still, never let a plant remain pot-bound.

Assemble Your Ingredients

Don't repot plants from tiny shacks to mansions; they're not the Beverly Hillbillies. Choose a new pot that's about one to two inches wider at the top than the previous pot. This will provide enough extra room without overwhelming the plant. Make sure the pot has holes on the bottom. Without holes for drainage, the roots will rot. Be sure to use a good commercial potting soil.

The Big Move

About an hour before you repot, water the plant just enough to moisten the soil. This keeps the soil together and lessens shock to the plant. If you're repotting inside the house, spread some newspaper around — lots.

commercial potting soil: a mixture of decomposed vegetable matter, wood fiber and vermiculite (highly water-absorbent silicate material), sold in 5-, 10- and 25-lb. bags by groceries, nurseries and other retailers

When you're ready to take the plant out of its pot, be patient and gentle. Spread your fingers over the soil, tip the plant upside down and tap the pot on the edge of a table. The plant should fall into your hand. Keep tapping the pot and lightly wiggling the plant until it comes free. You may need some help with larger plants. Have a bribe in mind when you ask.

GOING TO POT

When you repot a plant, make sure the new pot has drainage holes. If you want a more attractive container, put the plant and its pot into a second container. You can use baskets, big vases, a bean pot, a letterbox — use your imagination. For plants in porous containers, you can buy clear plastic trays that will hold drainage.

Put a layer of soil in the new pot and stick the plant in. The plant's base, the level at which it grows out of the soil, should sit about an inch lower than the pot's rim. Once you've got the plant at the right level, fill soil in evenly all around it. Make sure there are no air pockets by firming the soil into tight spaces with a chopstick or screwdriver. Put some fresh soil over the existing soil, but don't bury the plant's base. Press the plant in lightly so the soil is firmly in the pot, but not compacted like cement. If it's too tight, water won't penetrate, and you'll have to pot it again.

Spread the branches evenly around the pot, and let the plant toast its new home with a good drink of water. Don't fertilize for about a month; the plant needs to adjust to the shock of moving.

Repotting large trailing plants can be like wrestling an octopus. If you get frustrated or things get really wild, just open your mouth and wail like Lucy Ricardo does when she's in a jam. I promise you'll feel better. You may even start laughing.

Some Other Activities for Fun

If you'd like to keep a plant in its original pot but still want to give it breathing room, be brave and get out the knife. You're going to have to trim the root mass. Take the plant out of its pot and cut slices off the sides and bottom of the root mass. Use a quick, clean motion; don't saw the roots. This may seem painful, but the plant will rebound. Wash the original pot and put the plant back in, filling the new space with soil.

Propagating

The Best Plants in Life are Free

Hanging plants need lots of pinching to keep them looking good. But you do get a bonus from all this work: you can propagate the parts removed and get new plants!

Propagating houseplants is rewarding and fun. I'm amazed that you can take a piece of a plant and it will grow into a separate plant. You can watch it happen. One minute a cutting is resting quietly in water, and the next, roots begin to form. After you move the cutting to a pot, it sits in the soil while the roots have a field day underground. Then suddenly there's new growth on the cutting — and before you know it, you've got another plant to take care of. Or give away. Houseplants make good gifts. Houseplants that don't cost anything make *great* gifts.

1. Stem Cuttings

The term *stem cuttings* is found in most books on propagation, but the truth is, they usually refer to *branch* cuttings. Most vines are propagated this way. Choose a healthy, young branch with a growing tip at the end. Use sharp scissors to make a clean cut; bruised ends may not root. Carefully remove leaves from a few inches of branch above the cut, so they won't be under water or soil when rooting.

Stick the branch in soil or water to root. If you root directly in soil, you can dust the stem end with rooting hormone powder. This will help it root faster, but isn't necessary. Keep the soil moist at all times so the new roots don't dry out. Branches rooted in water can be put into pots when about two inches of root have developed.

rooting hormone powder: found at plant stores and nurseries, this powder accelerates root growth in plant cuttings rooted in soil

Put several propagated branches into a pot so the new plant will look full more quickly. One newly rooted Wandering Jew growing in a pot doesn't make a particularly stunning plant.

2. Root Division

Some plants don't propagate well from cuttings. You get new plants by dividing up the main plant's root mass. This takes a sharp knife and some faith. It's one thing to cut a branch off and root it; it's another to chop the whole plant up.

Take the plant out of its pot and examine it at the point it grows out of the soil. There may be distinct sections that can be cut, or you may just need to cut the plant into equal pieces. Divide the foliage so that you can use a large, very sharp, carving knife to cut through the plant and the root mass. Press down to make a clean cut, rocking the knife a bit if necessary. Don't saw the roots; this will bruise them. Plant the sections, keeping the plant bases at the same soil level as the original plant.

GO EASY ON THE BABY FOOD

You wouldn't give a baby a pepperoni pizza with extra cheese. Even though a newly propagated plant is in a regrowth phase, don't feed it for a few months; you can overfertilize it and burn the young roots. Once the plant has been actively growing for a month, give it a weak dose of fertilizer, about one-quarter to one-half the recommended strength. You can begin feeding the new plant regularly after its first birthday.

Propagating the Heartleaf Philodendron. Heartleaf Philodendron vines have visible bumps, or nodes, that will develop into roots. Put three- to four-inch stem cuttings in water and pot when roots develop. Or stick cuttings directly in soil, keeping it moist to help roots grow.

Propagating Grape Ivy. Propagate Grape Ivy from young, green stem cuttings, not the woody sections. Put cuttings in water and plant when roots develop. Or root cuttings directly in soil, keeping it moist to help roots grow.

Propagating Hedera Ivy. Hedera Ivy vines have small bumps, or nodes, that will develop roots. Stick short vine cuttings in water and plant when roots develop. Or put cuttings directly in soil, keeping it moist to help the roots form.

Propagating the Arrowhead Vine. This plant is easy to propagate from stem cuttings. Put cuttings in soil, keeping them moist to help roots grow. Or put cuttings in water and plant when roots develop.

Propagating the Creeping Fig. The Creeping Fig is propagated by stem cuttings. Root short cuttings in water and plant when the roots develop. Or put cuttings in soil. Keep the soil moist to help roots form.

Propagating the Button Fern. Propagate by root division. Take the plant out of its pot and cut it into sections with a sharp knife. Be sure each section has roots and a few fronds. Plant each section separately.

Propagating the Asparagus Fern. Use root division to propagate, a common technique for a pot-bound plant. Separate the foliage and cut through the root mass, leaving roots and branches in each section. Plant each section separately. New branches will sprout from the root mass.

Propagating the Wandering Jew. This is easy to propagate from stem cuttings. Put short cuttings in water and plant when roots develop. Or stick cuttings directly in soil, keeping it moist to support root formation.

All Things in Time

Propagating plants is an amazing process of regeneration, so be patient. It takes anywhere from three to six weeks for a cutting to develop roots. Then it takes time for the rooted cutting or replanted division to send out new growth. Baby plants also need a little while to get over separation anxiety from the mother plant. Once they're potted, water them regularly and forget about them. When you're not looking, they'll suddenly turn into healthy, growing young plants.

Pests and Diseases

Uh-oh...

Humans can definitely screw up a plant's day if they don't provide proper care. Over-watering, underwatering, too little light or too much fertilizer can all cause problems. House-plant pests and diseases are a separate problem. They're not usually our fault, but they are more troublesome because of the additional care needed to deal with them.

Most of these eight Handsome Hanging Plants are not susceptible to diseases and are vulnerable to only a few common pests; descriptions follow.

Fungus Gnats

Almost any plant can get gnats, sometimes called mushroom flies. These slow little bugs hover over the soil. They aren't harmful, but they are obnoxious. Insecticide applied to the soil will control them.

Scale

All plants are vulnerable to scale. When young, the brown or yellow insects move around the plant, but as they get older they get a hard shell and cling like barnacles to leaves and branches. They suck sap and excrete a clear, sticky substance. Rub scale off with a swab dipped in rubbing alcohol, and remove badly infected plant parts. Insecticides can also help.

Mealy Bugs

These white, quarter-inch-long bugs wrap themselves in a wool-like substance that repels water and contact insecticide. They suck sap and cause leaves to drop. Rub off bugs with a swab dipped in rubbing alcohol, and remove badly infected parts. Systemic insecticides can also help. Grape Ivy, Hedera Ivy and the Button Fern are vulnerable.

Spider Mites

These tiny ticks are so small you can't see them, but you can see the tiny webs on the undersides of leaves. Mites suck sap, causing leaves to be mottled and dry, and stunting new growth. Regular, strong misting and increased humidity can keep them in check. Insecticides help, but mites are hard to eliminate. Grape Ivy and Hedera Ivy, Creeping Fig and the Asparagus Fern are susceptible.

Whiteflies

These are tiny moth-like bugs that sit on the undersides of leaves. They suck sap and excrete a clear, sticky substance. Translucent larvae can be found in masses on the leaves' undersides. Contact insecticides will kill larvae; systemic treatment is needed to treat the adults. Whiteflies are hard to eliminate. Hedera Ivy and Asparagus Fern are vulnerable.

Many pests can be destroyed by washing the plant in mild sudsy water, about one teaspoon of soap or mild dish detergent to a gallon. For hanging plants, fill a spray bottle with this solution and spray both sides of the leaves. Then rinse the leaves in the shower so the solution won't injure the plant. Cover the soil with plastic wrap or foil so the solution doesn't get into it. Do this once a week for two or three weeks until the infestation has cleared.

Contact insecticides are sprayed onto the plants and the bugs. Systemic insecticides are applied to the soil or onto the plant's leaves and work through the plant's sap. Talk to staff at a gardening store about the best treatment.

Bring in a sample of the sick plant to help them determine what the problem is.

Insecticides are poisons; follow the instructions on the product's label carefully. If you're uncomfortable with insecticides, there aren't too many options. It's better to get a new plant than risk infecting all of your plants.

An Ounce of Prevention

Houseplant pests can be discouraging. The earlier you catch them and begin treatment, the better luck you'll have in saving the plant.

TRY NOT TO MAKE
THE SAME MISTAKE TWICE

Sometimes all you can do with a bad pest situation is throw the plant away. But try to figure out how it got infected.

- Was it a new plant?
- Where did you buy it?
- Did you keep the plant clean?
- Did you remove any weak portions?
- Had it been outdoors for awhile, or was it near an open window where bugs could have come in?

You may never know, but identifying a potential cause may help you avoid similar problems with a new plant. And don't be discouraged; pests happen.

Give your plants a little check-up once in awhile, looking for signs of trouble. Keep plants strong and resistant by cleaning them and removing withered leaves. And always keep a sick plant away from healthy plants!

HANGING OUT — OR TRAINING UP

Hanging Out

To really appreciate the flowing character of a hanging plant, its branches or vines need to — hang. But how do you get that English Ivy above your head, and make sure it stays there? It's no fun to clean up a plant that's done a half-gainer onto the kitchen floor.

Hanging your plant calls for the heavy equipment: hammer, screwdriver or maybe even an electric drill. These basic tools are enough to get your plant firmly attached to a wall or ceiling.

Go for the Interior Decorating Award

Wall brackets intended for hanging plants are available at nurseries and hardware and discount stores. The brackets have arms that extend the pot beyond the wall; they often swivel to give you flexibility in positioning the plant.

If your glorious Asparagus Fern demands a focal point in a special place away from the wall, you can use a ceiling hook. You can buy a plant hook that rotates to help you turn the plant for even growth.

There are poles that have arms to hold several plants. Some arms have pedestals; the plants rest on them and drape down without the need for a hanging hook. These poles are held between floor and ceiling by a telescoping spring action, or have a heavy base to keep the pole from toppling.

Or solve the problem by setting the plant on a pedestal table, usually about four feet high, to keep long branches from hitting the floor.

Make Sure Breaking Up Is Hard To Do

Whether you're hanging something from a wall or the ceiling, make sure the plant's weight is fully supported. Use screws, not nails, to anchor the hardware firmly to a stud, or use molly screws in dry wall or plaster. These ingenious fasteners go into the dry wall and spread "arms" on the other side of the wall to spread the load and prevent the wall from crumbling. Talk to staff at your handware store about the weight of your plant, where you're hanging it and how to keep it there.

When Bad Pots Happen to Good Plants

Many hanging plants are sold with plastic or wire hooks inserted into the pot's rim. These pots are functional, but not stunning. One option is to buy plant hangers with little hooks to insert into the holes in the pot's rim. These are usually made of rope, wooden beads, chain or other materials that complement foliage. The benefit of these hangers is that they take advantage of the hanging pot's design, which has a drainage saucer attached.

If you want to use a different pot, make sure that it has drainage holes and an attached saucer. Otherwise, excess water will immediately drain onto the floor. Pots not designed for hanging won't have holes in the rim, so you'll need to use a "cradle" hanger that wraps under the pot and connects to the hanging hardware. Cradles are usually made of rope or netting material, and are one of the few still socially acceptable uses for macramé. They can also hold a separate drainage saucer.

The More the Merrier

If you are hanging a vine, consider planting

several plants in a pot large enough to hold them, to achieve a better effect.

Go Climb a Tree (or a Wire Form)

If you have a history of brown thumb syndrome, you might be perfectly happy if you've managed to keep your trailing plant trailing, rather than expiring. But you should know that these plants can do more than just hang around. If you want a more formal look, have a knack for sculpture or are just a control freak, you can train your vine to climb on a form.

The natural tendency of many trailing plants is to grab hold of something and start growing in that direction. Some plants sprout aerial roots from the vines, and others have gripping tendrils. Both allow the plants to hang onto a surface, and you can help the process by providing one.

A Little Something to Grow On

There are different supports you can use to train plants. The Philodendron and Arrowhead Vine have aerial roots. These do better on a support that's covered in a moist growing medium, such as moss. If left to trail, aerial roots take moisture from the air. If they get near wet moss, the roots will burrow in and act like underground roots, pulling moisture from the moss and support-ing the plant on the form.

You can buy pieces of wood or wire forms that are covered in sphagnum moss at plant nurseries and craft shops. You can also cover wire forms yourself, or roll a cylinder of chicken wire and pack it tightly with moss. Make sure whatever form you use is sturdy; once plants start climbing they can get very big. Leaves on a climbing Philodendron are often much larger than on one that's trailing.

> sphagnum moss: a highly absorbent moss that is grown on fresh-water ponds and sold dry at plant and craft stores

Once you've got a form, anchor it in the pot by bracing it with a couple of heavy rocks and then filling the pot with soil and plants. A few small plants work better than one plant. You may want to use a bigger pot to weigh things down; a climbing plant can get top-heavy. Pin the vines to the moss with hairpins or wire bent into a U-shape, and watch your plant start climbing like a monkey! Spray the moss with water every day; the aerial roots will depend more on the moss than the soil for moisture. And keep the plant away from heat sources.

Something Else to Grow On

Trailing plants that don't have aerial vines such as Hedera Ivy and Creeping Fig can be trained to climb supports without a growing medium. You can use wire forms and trellises, simple bamboo canes or rattan stakes. All are available at plant and craft stores. Or create your own forms out of stiff wire — and practice for the day when you build flower-covered floats for parades.

Firmly anchor the form into the soil with the plant and attach the vines or branches to the form. You can use thin florist wire, twine or twist ties (the kind that come with plastic bags). Wrap the wire firmly around the vines — enough to keep the plant attached to the form but not so tight that the vines will be choked as they grow thicker.

Plants like Hedera Ivy that have tendrils will eventually grip a form by themselves; you just may need to help new growth get attached now and then. The Creeping Fig doesn't have tendrils and is completely dependent on being wrapped around and attached to the form.

Climb Your Way to More Versatility

Training trailing plants to climb expands their decorating potential. Essentially, you're taking a plant that falls downward and turning it into an upright plant. It's like taking long hair and piling it into a beehive 'do, only you're substituting florist wire for a half-gallon of hairspray. Fortunately, it will look a lot more natural.

This Would Look Divine in the Den

When you've decided to grow a hanging plant, it's because you have a particular look in mind. Hanging plants are similar in that they spread, flow, cascade, spill gracefully. They are different in color and texture. The Asparagus Fern is soft and billowy, while the Heartleaf Philodendron is more sedate and traditional. A Grape Ivy has a dark, heavy presence; the Button Fern is more dainty. Use these characteristics to fit the room they'll be living in.

First Things First

Before you settle on a plant and a room, look at the growing conditions. Is there enough light for the plant you want? If not, consider a different plant for the location, or another location for the plant. Are you thinking of putting a Creeping Fig on a credenza in the entryway? A couple of cold blasts from an open door and you might be creeping to the trash can with a dead fig.

He Had So Much Potential...

The unique character of trailing plants provides many opportunities for being creative. It seems a waste to see a long trailing plant with its branches just lying across a table. Trailing plants are meant to drape, spread, billow and hang; let them exercise their full potential. If you've got a big square end table that looks bare underneath, let a Hedera Ivy spread its limbs and fill the space. Maybe you want privacy in your bathroom, but don't want to put up a clumsy shade. A bushy Asparagus Fern will add privacy without blocking too much light. The Grape Ivy covering my stereo speaker makes it seem like the sound is coming from a hidden, built-in source.

A TRAIL MIX OF DECORATING TIPS

- A few small Button Ferns will add life to an entertainment center.
- Grape Ivy can fill the awkward space between cabinets and the ceiling.
- An Arrowhead Vine can trail along a fireplace mantle.
- English Ivy trained around a door makes a romantic entryway.
- A Creeping Fig on a pedestal gives a room a very classical feeling.

How High Can You Go?

The ability to let trailing plants hang presents an interesting question: how high should you hang a plant? I often see a Wandering Jew in a pot up near the ceiling, with a few short

YOU NEED TO GET OUT ONCE IN A WHILE

Many people put hanging plants outside during the warmer months. Hanging plants on a deck or screen porch look great, and make the space feel cooler. But get them used to the great outdoors gradually. First make sure it's warm enough both day and night — and take plants inside if you get a night below 55°. If their final spot will be in the sun, start them in the shade and move them every few days into brighter light. And when everyone's wearing fall sweaters and it's time to bring them back in, check carefully for pests. You could be bringing more than the plants into the house!

branches barely making it over the rim. All I can think is, "Gee, nice pot."

Think about what you see when a plant is hanging. Some are full enough or have large enough leaves that they'll look good from any height. But you don't want to look at the undersides of leaves and branches. I don't mean to sound superior, but the way a Button Fern grows, it should be looked down on — meaning set at eye level or lower. The same is true for a Creeping Fig, since it tends to spread outward. If it's placed up high, the only one seeing its best side is the fly on the ceiling.

When you're hanging a plant, test it at different levels. Start at eye level and keep moving it up six inches or so. You'll see that one minute it looks good, the next you get the sense of peeking up under its skirt.

• • •

The great thing about houseplants is that with very little effort, you get something that soothes, enriches and energizes your life. You don't have to chant or light incense or give up dairy products. You just live with them and give them a little care. So get your hands in the dirt. Feel the cool smoothness of the leaves. Watch them grow. And admire that lovely green thumb you've developed!

BIBLIOGRAPHY

Brookes, John. ed. *House Plants.* RD Home Handbooks. Pleasantville, NY: The Reader's Digest Association Inc., 1990.

Graf, Alfred Byrd. *Exotica.* E. Rutherford, NJ: Roehrs Co., Inc., 1973.

Handyman's Houseplants Tips Page. World Wide Web, 1997.

Horticulture and Home Pest News. World Wide Web. Ames, IA: Iowa State University Extension, 1996.

"Plant Answers." *Aggie Horticulture.* World Wide Web. College Station, TX: Texas A&M University, 1997.

Seddon, George. *The Mitchell Beazley Pocket Guide to Indoor Plants.* London, England: Mitchell Beazley Publishers, 1979.

Taylor, Norman. *Taylor's Guide to Houseplants.* Rev. ed. Boston, MA: Houghton Mifflin Co., 1987.

Time Life Houseplant Pavilion. World Wide Web. New York, NY: Time Life, Inc., 1997.

INDEX